Wild Harvest

Edible Plants of
the Pacific Northwest

Terry Domico

Drawings by
Hannah Jones

hancock
house

ISBN 0-88839-022-X
Copyright © 1979 Terry Domico

09 08 07 06 05 04 03 02   10 9 8 7 6 5

Cataloging in Publication Data
Domico, Terry
 Wild harvest
 Edible plants of the pacific northwest

 Bibliography: p.
 ISBN 0-88839-022-X

 1. Wild plants, edible—Northwest, Pacific—Identification.
2. Poisonous plants—Northwest, Pacific—Identification.
3. Cookery (Wild foods). I. Title.
QK98.5.N6D64   581.6'32'09795   C78-002106-1

Published simultaneously in Canada and the United States by

HANCOCK HOUSE PUBLISHERS LTD.
19313 Zero Avenue, Surrey, B.C. V3S 9R9
(604) 538-1114 Fax (604) 538-2262

HANCOCK HOUSE PUBLISHERS
1431 Harrison Avenue, Blaine, WA 98230-5005
(604) 538-1114 Fax (604) 538-2262
Web Site: www.hancockhouse.com *email:* sales@hancockhouse.com

Contents

Introduction

Food itself means basic animal existence, but wild food is food for our imaginations as well as for our bodies. When kneeling in some forgotten field pulling roots or eating tender spring leaves or standing under the canopies of conifers, delicately stripping off huckleberries and spruce buds, I sometimes become aware of a second person in me. My body is ten thousand years in the past, feeling dim memories; my mind embraces ten thousand years of future. I call this phenomenon, which springs from the satisfaction of the hand-to-mouth experience, grazing.

The popularity of eating "weeds" and wild things is growing. Most people indulge in it as a game, but the game has considerable survival significance. It makes us more aware of the whole woods. In a society that generally turns its back on the natural and biological environment, this natural exposure is especially desirable and useful. This fieldbook and guide to some common wild edible plants found around the Pacific Northwest is written, then, with that potential grazer in mind.

Most items in this fieldbook are arranged according to season. Seasons, with the possible exception of fall, are generally transitional in the Pacific Northwest. Since many plants may lag in their development during cold or windy weather, I hope that new grazers will find these divisions to be elastic guidelines for the seasons.

Many plants are considered edible simply because we can eat them without becoming ill. The standards of edibility should be raised, however, as some of these so called edibles offer very little in nutrition and taste. I have excluded a number of them from these pages for that reason. My own bias and ignorance have led to the exclusion of some plants, and, as a conservation measure, a few plants that are both edible and rare have been omitted in this work because they may be fast disappearing from our woods and fields.

The purpose of this book is to offer the initiate a useful tool for the identification and uses of wild edible plants. The photographs and drawings show the plants in their most desirable stages. I hope that, taken together, they will furnish positive identification for the new grazer. To the specialists and enthusiasts already deep within the pastures, I offer fellowship.

Spring

Weeks of pregnant buds and budding ideas.

Stinging Nettle, *Urtica dioica*

One of the first new green plants to appear in our woods, stinging nettles sometimes are found as early as February. The entire plant is thickset with a furry covering of small, needle-shaped hairs. Each hair is equipped with a rubbery bulblike base. A hapless hand or leg brushing them gets a minute dose of irritant which produces a prickly, burning sensation. The skin becomes super-sensitive. To some, this feeling is almost pleasant. You may get this tingly rash if you pick them carelessly. Nettles were popularly eaten in merry old England and are still popular in many European country kitchens.

The tender tops and shoots are best for greens. Pick them, using gloves or caution, by pressing the fine hairs downward against the stem and pinching.

Cook these tops like spinach, parboiling a few minutes to destroy their sting. Be sure to cook until completely wilted. Serve smothered in butter. Save the juice, for it makes a robust tea rich in minerals. Dried leaves can be stored for tea or added to soups.

By summer the plants become too tall and coarse for good eating.

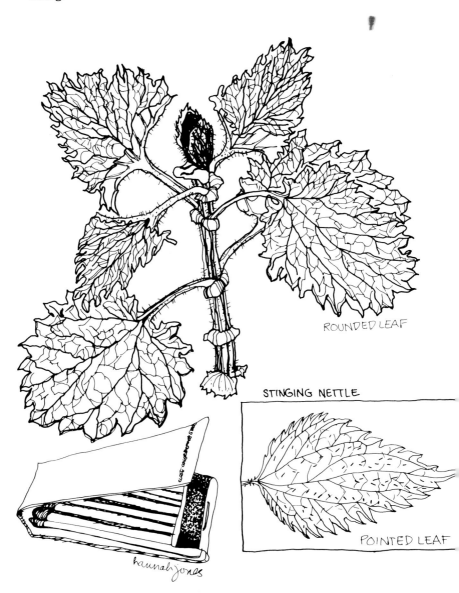

ROUNDED LEAF

STINGING NETTLE

POINTED LEAF

hannah jones

Oregon Broad-Leaf or Bigleaf Maple, *Acer macrophyllum*

The leaves of this moss cloaked monarch of the second growth woods are very large, six to twenty-three inches in diameter, dark green and shiny. The bark is graybrown, thin, smooth, and on big trees, vertically pleated on the trunk.

As warm spring days with cool crisp nights start to appear, the maple begins a new season by sending sap up into its budding branches. During these warmer days you can catch this sap and convert it into syrup to sweeten your breakfast waffles. Start in early February, if you wish. Each tree will produce sap for a few days to a couple of weeks. Individual trees send the sap from their roots at different times, so it's best to proceed by experiment. On a really warm, sunny day when the sap is rising, maple trees will actually ooze droplets from the tips of the branches.

First drill a hole an inch or two deep and about three-quarters of an inch in diameter. Make the hole as close to the ground as possible, leaving room to hang the pail. The hole won't hurt the tree permanently; in about a year it will be completely grown over. Into the hole, drive a close fitting metal or plastic tube or spout to guide the sap as it drips out. Do not drive the tube all the way to the back of the hole but just far enough to secure it. There should be a collecting space for the sap behind the tube.

Hang a pail on the tube to catch the dripping sap and then cover the whole affair to protect it from diluting rain. The sunny sides of the tree do best but don't be dismayed if you hit a "dry well" occasionally. Sometimes a "gusher" will yield a gallon or two of sap during an afternoon.

Pour the sap into a wide-mouthed stainless pan or other suitable container and heat to 160 degrees F., or until steaming. Continue to heat but do not boil. Watch closely. This operation is best done in a well-ventilated kitchen or outdoors if you don't want condensed water dripping down on you! Our maples have a little more water in their sap than Vermont's, so we need a little more time and fuel.

When finished, a cooled tablespoonful of sap should be thick, amber, and very sweet. Remove the syrup from the heat and bottle. Three gallons or so of sap will make about a quart of syrup which, while as good as any maple syrup, will not taste store-bought.

The yellow flower-clusters that the early bees are so fond of make an excellent garnish for salads and may be eaten right from the tree. They are sweet with nectar, so be sure to shake out any bees before attempting to eat. Once, a salad produced a bewildered bee just as I was lifting a mouthful! These blossoms are good alone or as a salad with a little vinegar and oil dressing.

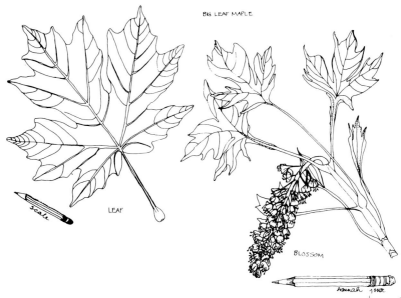

BIG LEAF MAPLE

LEAF

BLOSSOM

9

Giant Horsetail, *Equisetum* species

Horsetails are the only living members of a prehistoric family, some of which grew to the size of trees. They consist of hollow, grooved, and jointed stalks. They grow from perennial rootstocks and sprout green and early, growing from two to four feet high when mature. The giant horsetail, which prefers damp woods and gravelly hillsides, is very common in the Pacific Northwest.

In the very early spring, just after the ground has thawed, dig underneath last year's shriveled stalks. The future shoots are encased in brown sheaths in neat little clusters atop the long rootstock and very much resemble tubers. Peeled and added to salads or stews, they can be quite good.

By mid-February, the stalks may protrude through the ground. These are the reproductive shoots. The upper stalk and head can be eaten raw or boiled. The head is covered by many closely packed spore-producing cells. These must be peeled off to uncover the white, tender inner core. They don't taste as good as in the tuberlike stage, but they have a valuable mineral content.

This plant has another form of shoot that looks somewhat like minature evergreen trees. These sterile, unreproductive shoots emerge in April alongside the now-mature reproductive stalks which by this time have become too tough to eat. The photosynthetic activity of this later stalk provides the root stock with food. Scouring rush is the name commonly given these bristly shoots. They are not considered edible because of their toughness and grittiness; however, they can be especially useful to campers as efficient plate and pan scrubbers.

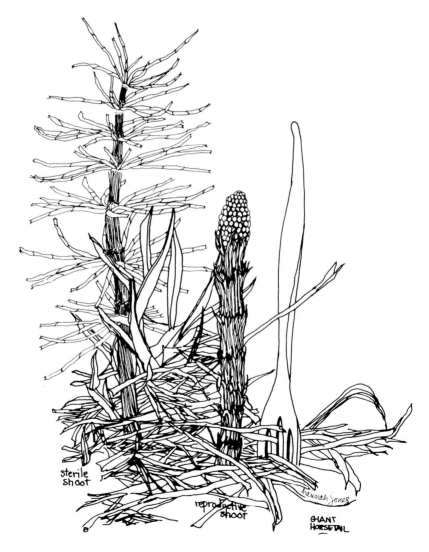

sterile shoot

reproductive shoot

GIANT HORSETAIL

Fireweed, *Epilobium angustifolium*

Fireweed is a tall herbaceous plant that springs up each year from creeping rootstalks. The brilliant rose-colored flowers and willowlike foliage appeal to both the eye and the palate. The name fireweed is apt because it springs up so quickly on burned-over areas often within two years after a fire. Rich stands on log slashes brighten many a bare and eroding hillside. This common plant grows in scattered clumps throughout its large coastal range. The tender young shoots are an excellent early pot vegetable—just boil a few minutes. A handful of the dried leaves, which brew up easily and have a fine flavor, will make a pot of tea.

The glutinous pith from the large summer fireweed stalks can be scraped out and either eaten raw or used in making delicious wild soup.

During the summer, I usually haul a few of our beehives up into a fireweed-rich area in hopes of obtaining that fragrant honey. If the bears don't wreck the hives, I'm often blessed. A few beekeepers around here make a good share of their living producing fireweed honey. It is light-colored and popular wherever sold.

Many Northwestern Indians used the fluffy seed cotton for wool substitute, mixing it with mountain goat wool or duck feathers, but these fluffs lack the qualities for really fine fiber.

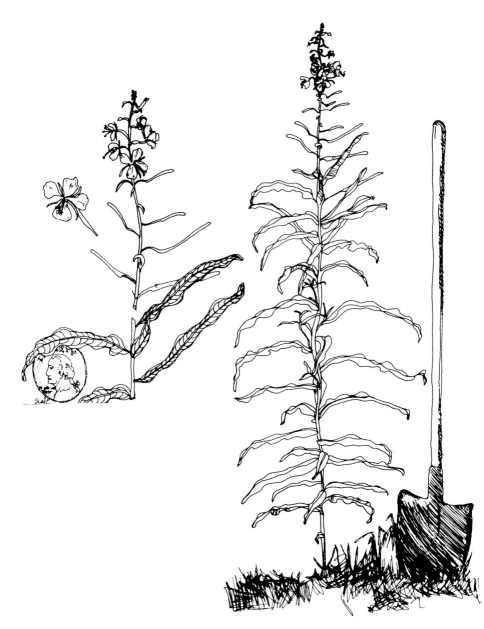

Sweet Coltsfoot, *Petasites speciosa*

Sweet coltsfoot grows in colonies in moist, shaded ground, preferring stream banks and the seeping ground of cut-banks.

Its flowers are borne in a pale purplish cluster atop the upright flower stalks that push up in early March. They appear just a bit ahead of its large unfurling leaves. These leaves rise directly from underground rootstocks and are supported by their own stems. The underside of the deeply cleft leaves is covered with a matted, wooly, white fuzz.

The leaf stalks and flower stems (with flowers) make a surprisingly tasty vegetable dish when freshly gathered. Prepare by cutting them into convenient pieces, about four inches long. Boil in enough water to just cover. After cooking for a few minutes, drain off the water and serve the vegetables topped with butter or sauce, asparagus style. It won't taste like asparagus, though. Its unique flavor can only be called coltsfoot.

Some northwestern Indians used coltsfoot in a cough medication. To make a similar cough syrup boil a large handful of the chopped leaves and stalks in just enough water to cover them. After a few minutes, pour off the liquid and sweeten with half a cup of honey. Simmer this mixture until it becomes syrupy when cooled. You may now bottle it and keep it refrigerated for medicinal use.

Finally, if you should be in want of salt some spring or summer day, you can make a substitute by drying and then burning coltsfoot leaves. This black and powdery preparation will provide a salty taste.

hannah jones

Siberian Miner's Lettuce, *Montia sibirica*

This succulent salad plant is usually found growing in the moist, open woods of the low-lying mountains or along streams. Its five- to twelve-inch-long reddish stems grow directly from a central "knot" and are arranged in a whorl around the base. Two kinds of leaves may be found on the same plant: lance-shaped basal leaves usually found prostrate near the ground, and a pair of opposite leaves form a "bow tie" on the erect flowering stems.

From late March into June many small five-petaled flowers are born. Each pink petal is streaked several times with red and every petal has a small notch at the apex.

Siberian miner's lettuce is very abundant in the coastal mountains from Alaska to California. It is a shy, retiring plant easily overlooked in a jumble of green.

The whole plant, excepting the fibrous roots, is edible. It can be cooked as a green, but it is probably best enjoyed in a salad. I prefer it coarsely chopped in a mixed salad topped with a light dressing. The leaves sometimes have a bitter tinge but the stems are generally sweet.

SCALE

hannah jones

17

Miner's Lettuce, *Montia perfoliata*

Many a succulent leaf and stemmed plant were known to the green-starved immigrants as miner's lettuce. This particular one, also called Indian lettuce, is easily recognizable by its five- to fifteen-inch stems which branch from the base of the plant, and by the leaves which form a shield at the summit of the stems. From the center of the leaf-shield a small stalk rises, bearing tiny white flowers from April through June.

It ranges in habitat from open moist woods to shaded fields. It seems to usually be associated with moisture. It is common in patches, especially on the Olympic Peninsula and San Juan Islands.

The leaves and stems may be eaten raw in salads or boiled as a potherb. As lettuce for sandwiches miner's lettuce may have no equal. The roots also are edible. When cooked, they have a nutlike flavor.

scale

hannah jones

19

Dandelion, *Taraxacum officinale*

The dandelion is very well known. It consists of a rosette of toothed, fleshy leaves surrounding a long taproot. Near the center of this rosette grow hollow stalks, each bearing a solitary, yellow, composite flower-head.

Unfortunately, the dandelion is usually considered a hostile weed in peoples' lawns and gardens. Eradication attempts are most often met with only partial success even though the hoe, the spade, and a host of deadly chemicals are brought into the fray.

The plant, transported by the early European settlers to many points over the globe, soon became firmly established in its new environs. Winged by its parachuted seeds, it quickly spread into almost every suitable habitat. I've read that it can even be found inside the Arctic Circle. The dandelion definitely has a life-hugging quality about it! It can reproduce, if necessary, without having to go through the bother of pollenization and fertilization by a process called parthenogenesis.

Dandelions do have many redeeming qualities, though. For

centuries the leaves have been eaten in salads and as a potherb. In many cases they were a good source of important vitamins in an otherwise deficient diet, particularly in the spring. The older leaves tend to be bitter, particularly after the plant has bloomed. Those growing in the moist shade seem to be the sweetest. When cooked properly as a potherb, the greens can be quite tasty. Bitter leaves can be sweetened by soaking them overnight in a bowl of water with a teaspoonful of baking soda thrown in.

The large amount of pollen gathered from the flowers is very important to the welfare of the bee colony. Occasionally, a fine-flavored honey made from the dandelion can be harvested from the bees. Many beekeepers rejoice when they see pastures and lawns covered with the bloom of dandelion.

Most winemaking guides offer one or two good recipes for some very good (and very strong) wines made from the flower's heads. When I was seventeen, a neighbor boy and I sampled some of his father's aging home-brew. I thought it quite good . . . Well . . . I was **very** late getting home that night!

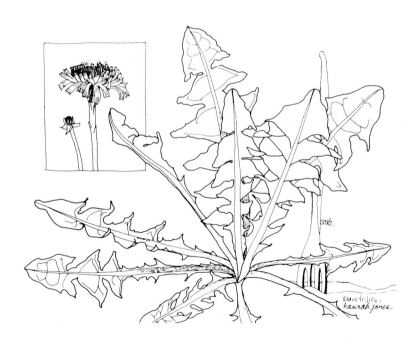

Dandelion.
hannah jones

Oso-berry or Indian Plum, *Osmaronia cerasiformis*

This is a very common shrubby plant with oblong leaves which are paler beneath. Oso-berry is one of the first bushes to bloom in the spring; at that time its musky flower clusters may be seen in almost every overgrown field and open wood. Oso-berry has separate male and female plants. Both have blossoms but only the female bears fruit. Its small white flowers seem to bloom for almost a month although they are soon obscured by quickening foliage.

In late June, its small fruits, about the size of cherry pits, ripen to a dusky purple. I think they are odd-tasting but pleasant, often having a distinctive plumlike flavor. The fruits fall from the bush quickly after ripening and are soon lost. This makes gathering them in quantity difficult. These berries dry well for winter use but I think the flavor is best if they are eaten when picked.

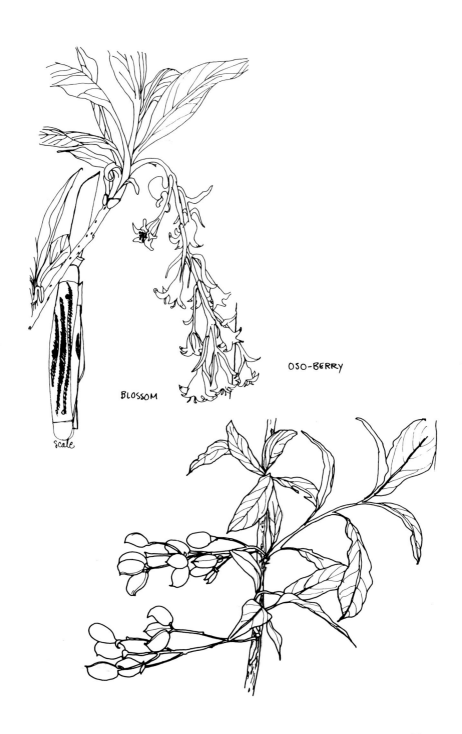

scale

BLOSSOM

OSO-BERRY

Mustard, *Brassica* species

Mustard is a stowaway immigrant from Europe by way of the early American settlers' seed bags. It is cosmopolitan throughout North America now, and can be found growing as a cultivated crop and as a weed on cultivated ground, in pastures, along roadsides and in semi-arid places. Almost any experienced farmer will recognize mustard when he sees it; as one puts it, "mustard's harder to get out than ticks on a dog's back."

This pretty little plant grows from two to four feet high and is characterized by its clasping upper leaves and bright yellow flowers. A planted field of mustard is an incredible, solid yellow. The plant is an annual which branches several times like a bush.

The whole seeds are useful in pickling spices, the ground-up seeds make an excellent sandwich spread; the plant is valuable for stock feed; and it makes one of the best cooked greens for humans. Simmer in a little water or steam.

scale

hannah jones

25

Bittercress or Peppergrass, *Cardamine* species

This is a common immigrant from Europe that really looks like a weed. In fact, few people in this country call it by any other name. Bittercress, or peppergrass, as I prefer to call it, is one of the many members of the mustard family. Many of the plants of this family look similar except for slight differences in their leaves, flower color or size. Most of them are edible to some degree.

Peppergrass is a small plant that is six to eight inches high. It is commonly found in gardens and yards or in open fields and along roadsides. A flowering stalk bearing leaves rises from the center of a basal set of leaves. It bears tiny white blossoms. The seeds form in long pods called siliques.

Traditionally, this plant is used in salads. Because of its hot radishlike flavor it might be wise to use it rather sparingly. Sprinkle the chopped greens over your food as a spicy condiment.

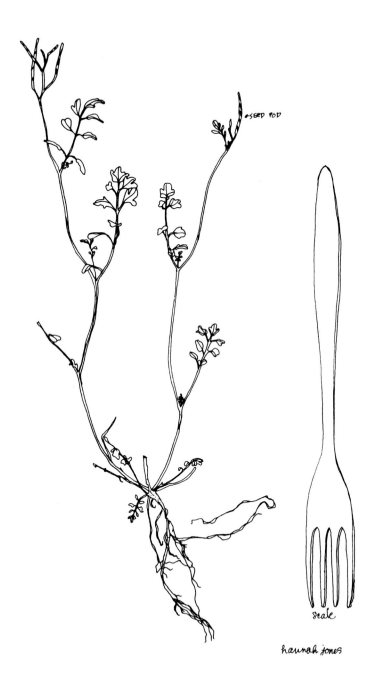

SEED POD

scale

hannah jones

27

Cattail, *Typha latifolia*

The cattail, or tule, as some folks call it, has a very wide distribution around the world. It is a lover of the margins of ponds and quiet streams and often is the dominant plant of marshes. Its name comes from the resemblance of its flower spike to the tail of a house cat. Cattails grow perennially, creeping rootstocks sending up new green shoots each spring. After the flower spikes have begun to ripen, the stalks and leaves wither and die. The fluffy spikes break apart and their seeds are carried away by the autumn and winter winds.

Many parts of the cattail are edible and quite nourishing. The rootstock is especially important because of the large amount of starch it contains. Dig it in the fall, winter, and early spring seasons. After washing thoroughly, cut into one or two-inch sections. Boil in water for five or ten minutes. Drain and then pass the cooked sections through a sieve to extract the starchy mush from the fibrous portion of the rootstock. This mush may be eaten or added to stew or soup as a thickener, or dried and ground for use as a flour.

One researcher reported that this flour contains about 57 percent carbohydrates.

In the springtime certain portions of the new leaves can be eaten. Grasp all of the two- or three-foot-tall leaves together and pull them loose in an upward motion. The leaves form a sheathlike bundle at their base. These tender bundles may be cut off for use in the kitchen. Soaked for awhile in vinegar they become very tasty instant pickles. Also, if the bundles are slit open with a knife, still more tender portions will be exposed. These can be boiled for a few minutes to be served as a delicious potherb seasoned and topped with butter.

The young green flower-spikes should be picked in the spring or early summer before the yellow pollen appears. Boil in a little salted water and eat like corn-on-the-cob, around the tough and wiry central core of the spike.

Incidentally, the pollen is good for enriching your flour. To gather it, simply place a paper bag around the flower spike, close, and shake vigorously.

Rose Hips, *Rosa* species

Rose hips are a very important source of vitamin C. These are the seed capsules formed in the fall by flowering roses. Indians gathered them to dry for winter use. The hips turn a bright red or orange by the beginning of winter and a few may survive until spring. Rose hips may be eaten raw (if you have no taste buds) or better yet, mashed and made into tea. A handful of rose hips will make a quart of delicious tea. Sweeten with a little honey.

If you want to make an excellent preserve from rose hips try rose hip marmalade. Add 2 cups of water to 1 pound of rose hips. Boil until tender, then pass through a sieve. Discard the seeds. To the resulting mash, add 1 pound of honey and boil some more until it jells. This makes about 2 pints of delicious brown spread.

I have also tasted an excellent wine made from rose hips; it's a very pleasant way to take your vitamins.

Hannah Jones

Wild Violets, *Viola* species

Wild Violets are also reported to be a good source of vitamin C. They appear early in the spring and may be found throughout the summer. The first to appear are the violet blue variety; later, the common ones will have yellow flowers with small purple pansylike markings. This is usually a shade-loving plant found near the edges of woods or under overhanging bushes. Occasionally, however, they may be found in moist pastures or meadows.

The flowers and shiny green leaves do well in sprucing up spring salads.

Summer

The growing green rush is on.

Buttercup, *Ranunculus* species

Buttercups grow a rosette of deeply divided leaves with stems that form a bunch resembling miniature celery. The edible roots look very much like spaghetti, being both white and fat with starch. A flower stalk about a foot high develops in April and produces blooms of golden five-petaled flowers far into summer. The resulting seeds are armed with strong hooks which attach themselves to passing animals and people. They hitchhike for a wide distribution.

Buttercups are generally thought to be poisonous when eaten raw. They contain a volatile toxic agent that can be removed by boiling. I always cook this plant by boiling for five minutes, changing the water, and then boiling for another five minutes.

The cooked roots will have a rather bland, sweet taste. Chop up and cook with scrambled eggs, in stews; substitute for bean sprouts in chow mein, or sauté and mix into rice dishes.

Sorrel, *Oxalis oregana*

In the rain-soaked forests of the Olympic Peninsula and in other wet coastal woods these delicate forest floor plants grow. In some localities, several acres of their pleasing shamrock-shaped leaves may be seen nodding gently in a secretive breeze. The one or two inch leaves and the flowers are supported by unbranched, succulent, upright stems, four to six inches tall. At night the leaves fold neatly downward, forming a three-sided nightcap. The flowers which appear from May through June may be white, yellow, or shades of lavender. Those of the Olympic Peninsula are generally white.

The leaves and stems are very refreshing to chew on when you are hiking through the forest. They contain oxalic acid salts which give them a sweetish lemony taste. Cooked and sweetened to taste, the stems are remarkably similar to freshly cooked rhubarb, and can be used in place of rhubarb in sour pies.

Coarsely chopped sorrel usually improves a salad.

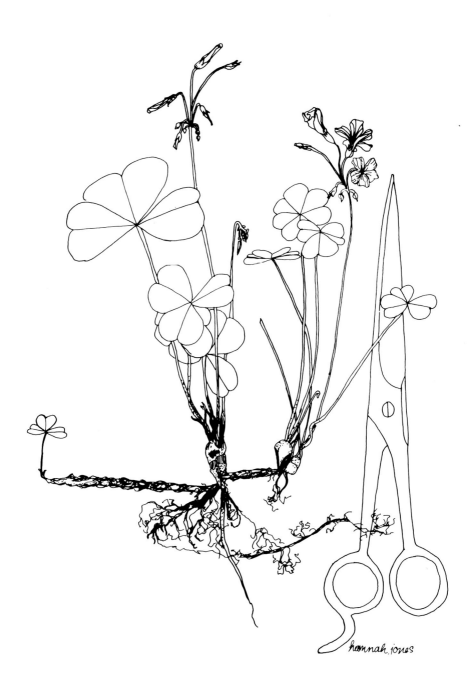

hannah jones

37

Glasswort or Pickleweed, *Salicornia* species

Glassworts are succulent, salty-tasting plants having leafless, jointed stems which resemble the scaly toes of chickens. Because of this resemblance, they are sometimes called chicken claws.

This plant is usually found growing in salty soil just above the high-tide mark in and around tide flats and saltwater marshes. It is a typical plant of the salty, low ground around Puget Sound, but can be found from California to Alaska.

The roots are perennial but the graygreen upper plant turns brown in late summer and withers away as the cold season approaches.

The best time to gather the plant for kitchen use is in the early summer or just before the numerous inconspicuous white flowers appear on its fleshy stems.

Glasswort stems make good pickles. Just boil them in fresh water for a minute or two and then soak them in any pickling brine. My favorite is the bread-and-butter sweet pickle type. After two weeks to a month of soaking in a sealed jar, your pickles should be ready.

Also, the fresh juicy stems are salty and are a pleasant addition to many salads.

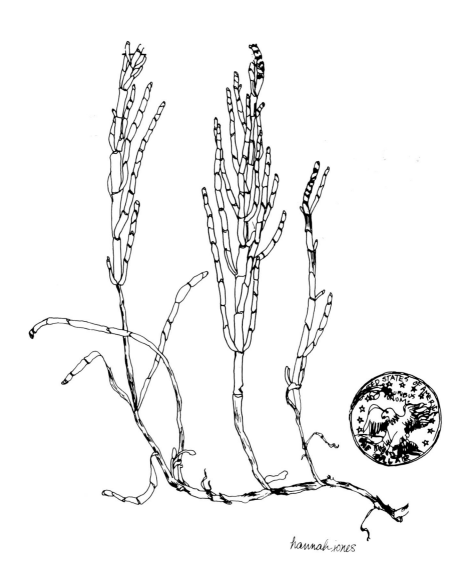

hannah jones

Western Wild Ginger, *Asarum caudatum*

Wild ginger is found in cool, moist, shaded woods, usually near a spring. The intertwining rootstocks are found just beneath the leaf litter and are anchored by numerous small roots. Its three to five inch leaves are almost heart-shaped and are a glossy deep green on the upper surface. The leaves grow directly from the underground rootstocks. In May and June, unique three-pronged, spidery flowers may be found half-hidden beneath the leaves. These beautiful lavender-red flowers are some of my favorites.

Use these rootstocks just as you would the commercial variety of ginger; dried, pulverized, and stored on your spice shelf. To gather ginger, simply dig the rootstocks with your hands, following the lines of leaves seen at the surface. To prepare, break off the leaf stems and small roots, then wash well in warm water. Ginger may be gathered the year around.

As a special treat, you may want to make some candied ginger. Cut the cleaned rootstalks into two-inch sections and boil them in heavy sugar syrup for about ten minutes. (1 cup of water to 1½ cups sugar will do.) When done, lift the sections with a fork onto a plate to cool and drain. The excess syrup may be saved for the next batch. When cooled, the candied sections should be tacky. Roll them in powdered sugar to separate the pieces for serving. In twenty-four hours the flavorful and exotic candy will have dried somewhat and may be kept in a closed container.

NOTE: Wild ginger grows rather slowly, in spreading colonies. Please be sure when digging their rootstocks to leave most of the colony intact. Otherwise they might disappear.

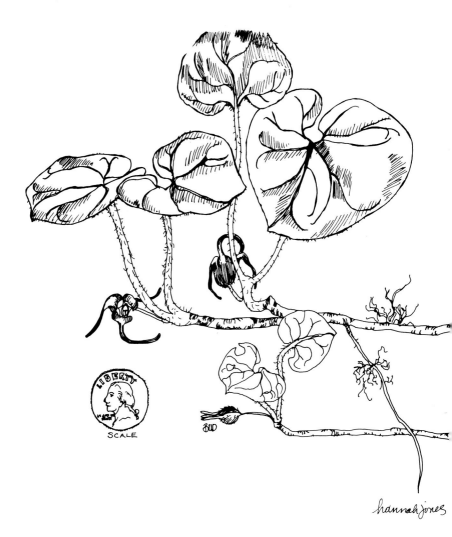

Clover, *Trifolium* species

There are several species of this plant in the Pacific Northwest, among them beach clover (*T. fimbriatum*), wild clover *(T. tridentatum)* and woolly-headed clover. Also, many introduced varieties grow in pastures and vacant fields. Together, they are an abundant food source. I consider the native clovers and the imported red clover the most useful. These plants grow from perennial, branched roots and have leaves which are divided into three leaflets. Their average height is about one foot. Flowers are borne in a complex head of varying colors according to the species, climatic conditions, and soil complexity. The flower color may range from white, yellow, or pink to deep red.

All parts of the plant are edible. If eaten in large quantity, they should be cooked to avoid any possibility of bloat or gas trouble. The stems and leaves can be cooked as a potherb.

A delicious tea can be made from the flower heads. To prepare, steep a crushed handful of dried tops in a few cups of hot water. Sweetened with honey; it tastes good and is good for you. To gather and store blossoms, pluck the tops during the peak of the bloom and stow them in a large burlap sack. Hang the sack in the sun or in a warm place indoors. They may dry in a week or so if they are mixed and stirred thoroughly each day. This insures even drying and prevents spoilage. A small amount can be dried in a warm oven.

The starchy roots may be dug anytime of the year but they are best during fall and winter. To prepare them for use, clean the large taprootlike portions of the roots well, removing smaller fibrous roots. (In some clovers even the large roots tend to be rather stringy.) Chop them into half-inch chunks and boil for five minutes or so in a panful of water. When done drain and season to eat as is or add to stew. They are bland and go well with spicy foods.

Red Sorrel or Sour Grass, *Rumex acetosella*

The basal leaves of the red sorrel form a rosette at ground level much like that of the dandelions. These narrow leaves are lobed at the base and look like arrowheads. Red sorrel is commonly found in exposed fields, neglected gardens and at the edges of lawns and roadsides. It is frequently used in European cooking, so it probably escaped from the early settlers' herb gardens. Now it seems to be naturalized and very much at home here.

In June and July, the plant sends up a fruiting stalk which in turn forms many small seeds. At this time the leaves turn a bright red. Later, they turn brown and dry in the heat of the autumn sun.

In the spring, and later, in moist places, the leaves will be green and quite tender. Their sour juice is very refreshing and goes well in a salad. Try adding them to good soups to make them better. The leaves dry well and retain some of their flavor, and, sprinkled generously, they will probably find good favor as a seasoning for meats, fish, rice and sauces.

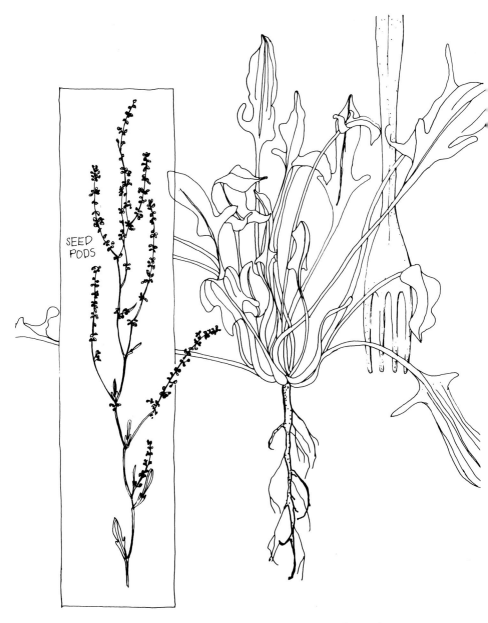

SEED
PODS

hannah jones

45

Lamb's Quarter, *Chenopodium album*

If you dig a garden in the Pacific Northwest, you are very likely to meet this tall, cosmopolitan herb from Europe. It loves the disturbed soil of the garden. The careful preparation, the weeding of grass and other undesirable plants, and the stimulating moisture from the watering hose waken the magical seeds of lamb's quarter, which seem to come from nowhere. Lamb's quarter has a coast to coast distribution. Often, it may be seen growing in patches along roadsides and other waste places. Sometimes it appears to be able to grow where no other plant can survive.

Lamb's quarter is an annual plant bearing distinctive leaves, each having a whitish or silver granular substance on the underside. The plant has a long stalk which in late summer and fall carries clusters of dark seeds near its summit.

The young leaves and tops are good in a salad, or cook them like spinach. To season, add a little vinegar just before serving. According to some sources, the greens have more nutritional value than spinach, and are especially rich in calcium.

Instead of planting spinach we cultivate these "weeds." When they are about six or eight inches high, they are just right for the pot. Lamb's quarter is an ideal garden plant, requiring neither planting nor care, and tastes better, to me, than spinach does.

In fall the dried seeds can be gathered and ground into flour. It enriches and adds variety when mixed with wheat flour.

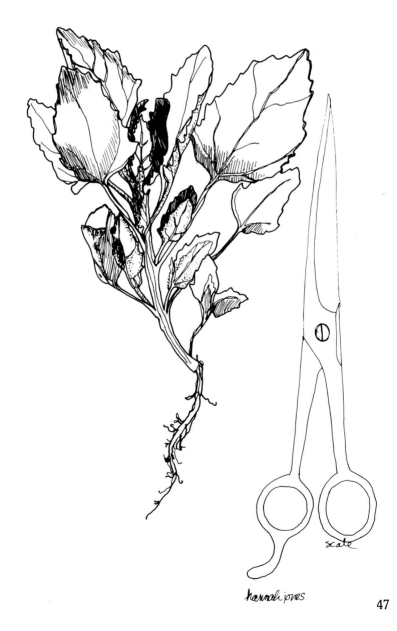

scale

hannah jones

Watercress, *Nasturtium officinale*

Growing in springs and slow-moving streams, this aquatic herb is best known as a salad plant. It is served in many restaurants and is sold in market places all over the world. In the United States, large areas of wetlands are used for its cultivation. In the Pacific Northwest it is usually found growing in wild colonies.

Watercress grows in floating masses anchored to the muddy bottom by white threadlike roots. It is at its best flavor just before it bears clusters of tiny white flowers at the apex of its stems. In the Pacific Northwest, it blooms around May and June, depending on the locality and altitude.

While very good for salads, this peppery plant can also be eaten cooked as a potherb.

NOTE: In the Pacific Northwest a very poisonous plant called water hemlock *(Cicuta douglasii)* shares the same habitat with watercress and, in its early stages of growth, may be confused with watercress. The leaves of water hemlock are more lance shaped and their margins are notched. Carefully compare your specimens with the drawing and photograph. Usually by the middle of May the water hemlock is noticeably taller than watercress, with stems growing from one to three feet in height. Watercress has a distinct peppery flavor.

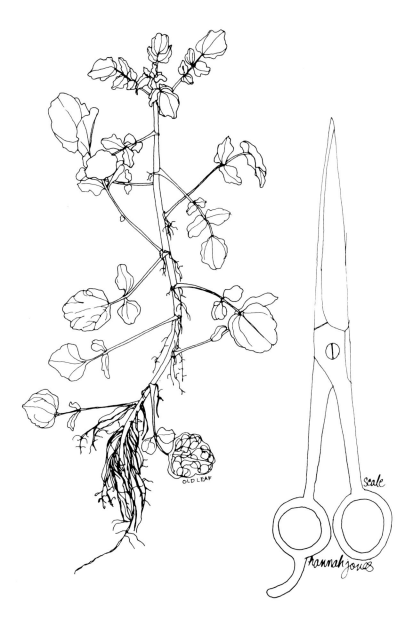

OLD LEAF

scale

hannah jones

Cascara, *Rhamnus purshiana*

Cascara is a tree which grows to a height of forty feet or more and bears heavily veined oval leaves. Its smooth, gray bark has been used for centuries by northwestern Indians as a very effective and gentle laxative.

Cascara bark preparations are still on the market and still seem to be one of the best laxatives. Commercial gatherers of the bark have found that when a tree is felled for its bark, the stump, if left intact, will usually send up two or more new saplings. Fortunately for the tree, a balance of conservation can be struck.

To prepare some of the medicine at home, cut and peel a stout limb from a good-sized tree. The bark should be dried naturally and is best gathered between spring and fall. The dry bark should be ground and pulverized. To use for relief of constipation, mix 1 level teaspoonful of the powder with 1½ cups of very hot water. When cool, drink the liquid tea.

Cascara, a species of buckthorn, is common through most of its range. It prefers the cool, moist, mixed woods from northern

California to southern British Columbia.

Around May, the tree bears inconspicuous green flowers. In the areas where cascara is particularly abundant, beekeepers sometimes harvest good crops of thick amber honey which had its origin in these small blossoms.

By August, its black cherrylike fruit is usually ripe and can be found hanging from single stems as late as the middle of September. Raw, they are mushy and contain several hard seeds. The cooked pulp can be separated by passing the mashed fruit through a coarse seive. The fruit is reported to be quite nutritious but it is usually too scattered about the tree for gathering in large quantities.

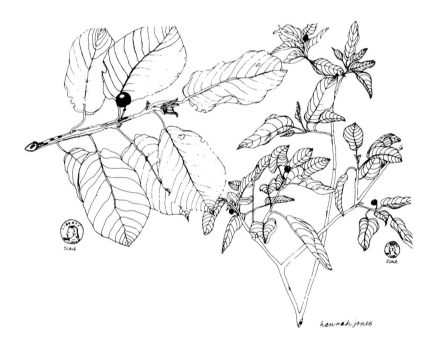

hannah jones

Wild Strawberry, *Fragaria* species

If the wild strawberry could sing a song, it would probably sound like "Pick me . . . picnic . . . pick me . . . picnic." The ripe, reddened fruit seems to invite you to stop and savor its sweet-tart juices.

There are four species found in the Pacific Northwest, all in poor soil. There is a beach variety, preferring sandy soil and dunes along the coast from Alaska to California. The other varieties prefer more upland terrain; open prairies, exposed fire scars, and warm, sheltered hillsides and meadows, particularly in the lower elevations.

Colonies of strawberries grow by sending out runners called stolons. Where these lateral branches touch the ground, a new plant forms and takes root. This habit tends to bind exposed soil, and so help prevent excessive soil erosion. New colonies spring up from undigested seeds dropped by birds or animals.

The white flowers have five petals with yellow centers. The berries ripen from May through July.

As a rule, the fruit of the wild strawberry is rather small, the largest berries the size of a thimble. But because of its fine flavor, I regard this small berry as the epitome of wild fruit. The domestic strawberry originated from this continent's wild stock. But somewhere in the production of the domestic variety much of the flavor and sweet scent was lost. It is these wild and rich flavors I seek to spice my everyday meals.

Occasionally, patches of ripe berries are extensive enough to warrant picking for future use. This addition to the freezer will be a delight to eat in the middle of winter.

A fairly good tea can be made by steeping a few green or dried leaves in a cup of hot water. Sweeten with a little honey or some ripe berries.

If you need food, the flowers, leaves, and green fruit are also edible, raw or cooked.

Thimbleberry, *Rubus parviflorus*

Thimbleberries, common relatives of the raspberry, grow best in open woods and may make up three to six-foot high thickets. They grow branched canes which do not die each year like our domestic raspberry. Each year in early spring the thimbleberry sends out new shoots and growth buds which, incidentally, can be eaten.

Later in spring, large, showy leaves appear. They are flat and five lobed with heavy veins—much like maple leaves. The plant blooms from late April until early August and produces a continuous crop of berries during the season. The flowers are quite large. Their white petals have a rumpled appearance as if they had been carried in a coat pocket.

The red berries form a cap and are quite seedy. When picked, they are very soft and mushy, and the juice stains the fingers red. I think they are quite tasty and find the seeds just add a pleasant crunch.

Because the berries don't seem to stand much handling, I've

never brought them into the kitchen. Reference sources say that they were dried into cakes by some of the northwestern Indians and that they are good as jelly and in pies.

thimbleberry

hannah jones

Salmonberry, *Rubus spectabilis*

After my introduction to this golden amber raspberry-like fruit, one of the first edible wild plants I had met, I concluded that they should be left to the bears and the birds. They have a sweetish, insipid flavor. But the salmonberry flavor grew with me. Now, I rarely walk by one of the fruit-laden shrubs without pausing for at least a few bites.

Salmonberry is one of the most common shrubs of the lower forests in the humid northwest. Its two to ten foot canes sometimes interlock to form almost impassable thickets, a common sight at the woods' edge. Once, when hiking off the trails, I was confronted by such a thicket. After a half an hour or more of thrashing through, I found myself gazing at a wall of thicket surrounding a small twenty foot clearing. I almost spent the night right there!

The reddish blooms have a rose-like appearance. They appear in April and may bloom through July. The first berries to ripen are in the lowlands and as the altitude increases they ripen progressively later. The berries themselves may range from honey orange to deep red in color.

The young tender shoots, as they emerged from the ground, were part of the diet of many northwestern Indian tribes. I chop the shoots coarsely and sauté them in butter. They lend themselves to casseroles and similar dishes but are just passable when eaten raw.

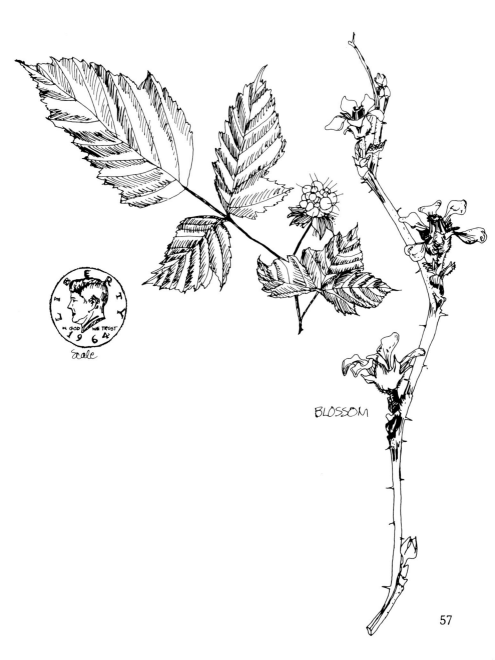

Scale

BLOSSOM

Red Huckleberry, *Vaccinium parvifolium*

A lover of shaded woods and second growth forest, this three to eight foot tall shrub can even be found growing on the tops of the mammoth tree stumps left by the early loggers. Red huckleberry is found in most lowland forests of the northwest.

It is usually recognizable by its small green leaves, lacey stems and red, tart berries. The round or oval leaves are about three-quarters of an inch long. Pale, inconspicuous flowers produce berries from late June until August. Sometimes the berries seem to be almost transparent. They provide glowing pink points even in the darkest of woods.

These berries are very good eating, raw or cooked. To pick them faster than the fingers can do, fashion a comb from some headless nails and a block of wood. Drive the nails partway in in an even row along one edge of the wood. The nails should be spaced a little less than the average diameter of the berries. Then just comb the berries from the bushes into a pail as bears do with their claws when they want to feast on berries. The few leaves and twigs that fall in with the berries can be separated later. You'll probably find you can pick quite a few berries in an hour.

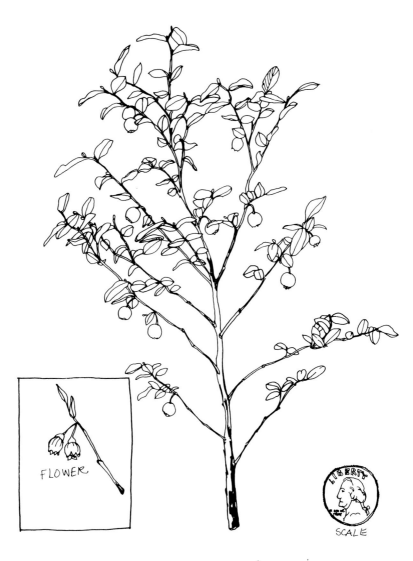

FLOWER

SCALE

hannah jones

Blackcap, *Rubus leucodermis*

These are distinctive and delicious blackberries which resemble the common raspberry. Like raspberries, they grow from biannual stalks or canes. The new canes are usually vegetative, bearing only leaves. In winter the plant will lose its leaves and become dormant until its second spring. The second year cane bears leaves, flowers, and fruit. The two canes may be found growing side by side, the younger one giving strength to the root, the older one fulfilling the age old contract of reproduction. The silvery canes are usually five or six feet tall, droop at the top, and are armed with sharp thorns.

July and August are the best months to find these berries ripe. Sometimes they can be found in abundance along open meadows and on exposed hillsides, especially a few years after a fire has burned the area. Unlike blackberries, which grow in dense thickets, blackcaps usually grow in clusters of three to seven upright canes.

The dark berry can be dried or prepared like any raspberry and is very good in pies and as jam.

Salal, *Gaultheria shallon*

In the lowland Pacific Northwest salal occurs as a typical undergrowth shrub. It bears evergreen leaves which are oval, up to four inches long, shiny on top, paler beneath, and minutely toothed. In sunny places, salal grows in dense, foot-high thickets. It tends to grow tall and spindly as the shade increases—from six to eight feet in height.

Salal's handsome, leafy branches are used extensively by florists. Year-around processing plants scattered throughout the Pacific Northwest give many woodsmen the opportunity to make some money and a quiet living picking brush.

Usually salal will show its pinkish bell-shaped flowers in June or July. In August, its dark purple fruit is ripe. These rough-skinned berries are good raw or cooked and also dry well for winter use. The natives used great quantities of salal berries mashed and dried, and made into blocks or cakes. These berries also lend themselves to jam and pies. Because salal berries are usually abundant and easy to gather, they have a growing popularity.

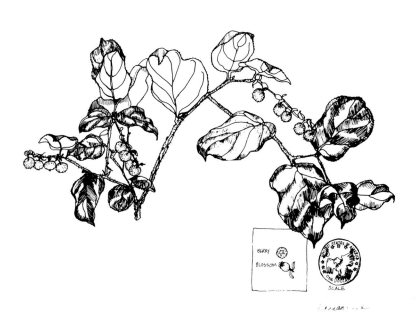

BERRY

BLOSSOM

UNITED STATES OF AMERICA
ONE DOLLAR

SCALE

Currants, *Ribes* species

The red-flowered currants bloom in April. Their deep-throated flowers offer nectar and hiding insects to the newly arrived hummingbirds.

There are several species of currants growing in the Pacific Northwest. Generally found in open woods, they are four to eight feet tall and bear lobed, palmately veined leaves. Some species have smooth stems while others are clothed with protective spines. Crossing through some patches of currants is like walking through a vegetable porcupine.

The blooming period of the various species is during the months of April, May and perhaps June.

The flowers are borne in slender, drooping clusters. Each species has its own particular color combination of flowers and fruit, which might be red, bluish, golden, or black. Currants of any color may be eaten, however some taste much better than others. Some varieties are downright insipid. Currants may be eaten fresh, dried like raisins, or cooked into good pies, mincemeats and jellies.

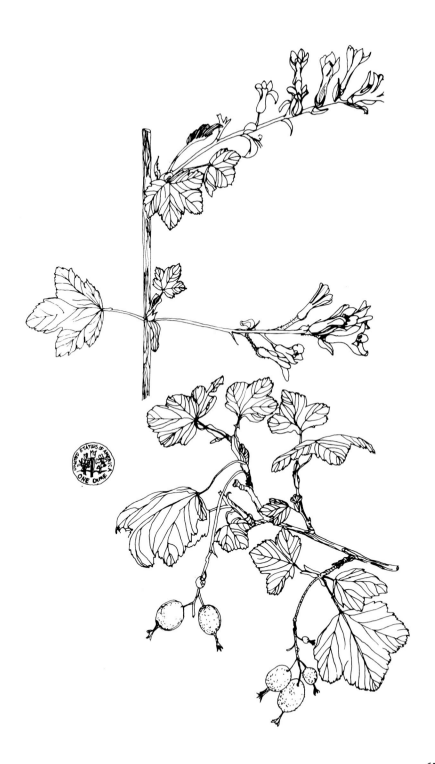

Trailing Blackberry, *Rubus macropetalus*

The symbol of summertime for me is the blackberry. Almost every country child sports scratch marks on his hands and legs from its prickly vines. Many people I meet in the woods bear a telltale purple thumb from picking its juicy berries.

There are three kinds in the Pacific Northwest. The trailing blackberry *(Rubus macropetalus)* is a delicate, creeping vine with small weak prickles. This variety seems to grow best on recently cleared land and on burned-over areas. Sometimes, within a few years after a logging operation is finished, it will cover the remaining logs, stumps, and rocks with a carpet of crisscrossing vines. A single branch may be up to twenty feet long.

Its flowers appear in May and June, and by July its sweet fruit is usually ripe. The female and male flower parts are found in separate flowers on separate plants. Only the small female flowers produce any fruit.

The Himalaya blackberry *(Rubus discolor)* and the evergreen, or split-leaf blackberry *(R. laciniatus)* are escapees from agriculture who found the climate to their liking. Almost everywhere in the lowland, in neglected clearings and farms and along fences, these large and aggressive plants grow. These blackberries usually form dense clumps or brier patches. Their stiff canes may reach fifteen feet high before they droop and finally trail back to the earth. Both varieties are heavily armed with large, stiff prickles.

Himalaya blackberry bears a large, juicy fruit which is usually ripe by early August. The evergreen blackberry matures a little later, in late August through September.

The fruit of blackberries is easy to preserve as jam or jelly or in the form of wine. I usually freeze at least a few quarts of the whole berries each year in the hopes of making pies during the winter.

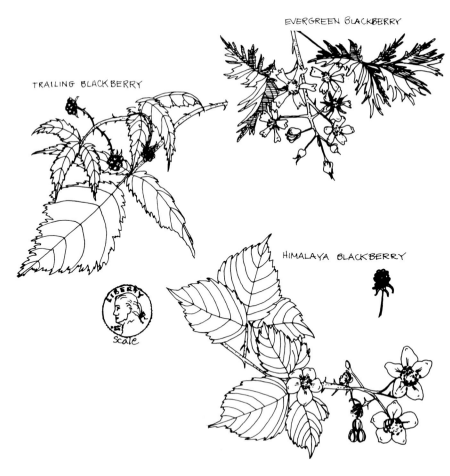

TRAILING BLACKBERRY

EVERGREEN BLACKBERRY

HIMALAYA BLACKBERRY

scale

Himalaya Blackberry, *Rubus discolor*

Evergreen Blackberry, *Rubus lacineatus*

Fall & Winter

Green things pulse slowly. Life's energy has been stored in seeds and roots.

Evergreen Huckleberry, *Vaccinium ovatum*

The evergreen huckleberry is a stout three to four foot tall shrub with reddish branches and small, evergreen leaves about one inch long, shiny on the upper surface and slightly toothed at the margins.

The species abounds in the open woods and on logged-off land in the lowlands of the Pacific Northwest, especially near the coast.

From May through July, pretty pink urn-shaped flowers appear. Numerous insects including bumblebees are attracted to these sweetly scented waxy flowers.

By the middle of August, most of the fruit will be ripe. In good huckleberry areas, great clusters of their dark berries can be found on heavily laden bushes. This and several related species are renowned for their heavy yields. Some are even grown or picked commercially.

The early settlers probably learned from the Indians that these berries dry well for winter use. They also adapted them for cooking in pancakes, muffins, pies, jellies, and syrup.

scale

hannah jones

Mountain or Big Huckleberry, *Vaccinium membranaceum*

This species can be found along the margins of partly shaded forest and in the logged-over areas that have been left to heal for a few years. It prefers altitudes ranging from two thousand to about five thousand feet. It is a small, branching, woody bush, one to four feet high. The stems have a reddish color and its small oval leaves have smooth margins. In autumn, the leaves turn infinite shades of orange and red. Occasional gusts of wind lift small clouds of leaves from this blazing mantle to turn and scatter them like storm-driven rain. By wintertime, the bare branches are covered with a quiet blanket of snow.

In the spring, fresh green leaves appear, and in late May, June or July, according to altitude, small urn-shaped flowers dangle like tiny lanterns.

Depending on the locality, its fruit will ripen around the months of July to September. It has rather large, dark blue berries which bear a bloom like some long-lingering frost. Many people call them blueberries and, indeed, they are closely related to the commercial blueberry. The jams, muffins, and pies the berries can be made into are as delicious as the berries fresh from the bush.

hannah jones

Oregon Grape, *Berberis aquifolium*

Oregon grape, the state flower of Oregon, is not really a grape at all but a member of the barberry family. It grows as a woody shrub, two to ten feet in height, and bears stiff, evergreen, hollylike leaves. Its favorite habitats are hillsides and open woodlands.

From March until May, its fragrant bright yellow flower clusters may be seen at the tops of its stems. These flowers and their buds are quite edible and are good in spring salads.

Oregon grape's dark blue berries ripen in the fall. Tart and lemony tasting, they are usually found in clusters and are covered with a heavy, powdery coating. These berries are famous for the fine wild-grape flavored jelly they produce. They also make a good pancake syrup when boiled in water and sweetened to taste.

The insides of the roots and stems, which Indians used for making dye and as medicine, are bright yellow. The boiled roots make a bitter tonic and appetite stimulant.

SCALE

Beaked Hazelnut, *Corylus* species

Before the first pussywillows shed their protective coats to model their spring furs, the hazelnuts begin to bloom. The long, yellow brown, sausage-shaped catkins appear in January or late February. These are the male flowers. In the warmer afternoon breezes, the mature catkins shed their pollen into the air. Studded along the branches wait the female parts, which hardly look like flowers at all. They are small, somewhat globular, and equipped with several sticky red filaments a quarter of an inch long which serve to trap the floating pollen.

By March the hazelnut bush puts on leaves and fades into the wooded thickets until fall.

The hazelnut grows into a bush five to fifteen feet in height and as big around. The nuts will be sweet and ripe in August, September, or October, depending on the locale. Watch the developing nuts closely if you plan to harvest any of their sweet meats, which are as good raw as roasted. In almost one day, the bushes will suddenly shed their twin, bristly husks containing two filbert-shaped nuts.

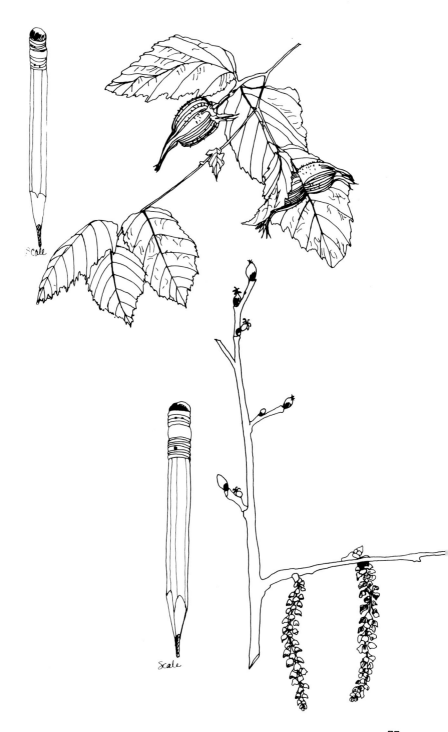

Scale

Scale

Madrona, *Arbutus menziesii*

One of the characteristic trees of Puget Sound is the cliff and bluff-loving madrona or arbutus which crowds the banks and beaches of the area.

Found at lower elevations, madronas average from thirty to seventy feet in height. They may be found growing in the coastal range from central California to southern British Columbia. They bear thick, oblong, evergreen leaves which are shiny green above and lighter beneath. The leaves are slowly shed and replaced during the summer. The tree's most unusual feature is its bark. In late summer, the red orange outer bark peels off in layers exposing new olive green bark beneath. Later, the silky-smooth new bark changes its character by turning to a deep red or orange. I love the contrasts during the shedding months—splashes of orange in a powerfully green landscape.

From April into May, the madrona offers white, urn-shaped flowers to all passing hummingbirds and bugs. Large bunches of red berries ripen from these blossoms in the fall. The berries are pea-sized or a little larger, and are covered with tiny bumps.

When raw, these berries are just barely edible. I prefer them boiled for a few minutes, drained of excess water, mashed, and then sweetened with a little honey for good measure. Prepared this way, you may find they taste like applesauce.

The berries dry well for out-of-season use. Cook them as you would fresh ones but boil them a few minutes longer to soften the fruit.

Because of their height, the mature trees which produce the most fruit are difficult to harvest from. The best picking may be found on steep hillsides where the uphill branches come close to the ground or near low banks on the beach. Often the action of the waves and wind will loosen the tree's grip on the earth and cause it to topple over the upper beach. Here, apparently supported by thin air, it may continue to grow. And here the beachcomber can reach its scarlet berries.

scale

Kinnikinnick, *Arctostaphylos uva-ursi*

Characterized by leathery, spatula-shaped leaves, this plant is an evergreen groundling of the Pacific forests. It occurs as a low growing, creeping shrub with reddish, woody branches only inches high. Since it prefers well drained, gravelly or sandy soil, it may be found growing in tangled mats in or near coniferous woods. Kinnikinnick is the Klallam Indian word for this plant, which many people may know better as bearberry. Bears are supposed to regard its bright red berries very highly.

The dried leaves were used as the principal ingredient in the smoking mixture of the northwestern Indian tribes. This mixture often contained dwarf bunchberry or dogwood leaves *(Cornus canadensis)* and the dry, pulverized leaves of salal. Many early writers of the Northwest tell stories about drunken sprees produced by swallowing and inhaling the smoke of this mixture. Because of these incidents, kinnikinnick garnered fame as a narcotic. Smoking dried kinnikinnick leaves had no effect on me, but it did smell like the downwind side of a smoky campfire.

The round berries, which ripen to a bright red, last well into the winter and may be dug from under the snow. The berry contains five or six hard seeds and is very dry, rather like a tough, tasty skin filled with flour. These berries are quite nourishing and contain very little starch. Cooking them brings out a better flavor but does little to improve their mealy dryness.

BERRY

Wild Cranberry, *Vaccinium oxycoccus*

The peat bogs around the shallow lowland lakes are the habitat of wild cranberries. Over many years, the growth of peat moss tends to fill lakes, forming thick mats of half-decayed material. The upper surface of the mats still grow, and adds to the mass which is partly floating on the surface of the lakes. Here the wild cranberries grow, trailing on top of the moss mats and twining through the branches of supporting bushes.

The plant itself is not much to behold, and may be overlooked. It is a delicate little vine with small stiff leaves that are dark green above and whitish beneath. The leaves are usually curled under at the margin. Pink flowers appear in June and July and hang pendent from threadlike stems.

By October, the fruit should be ripe but they do seem best after the first frost. Fresh cranberries have good keeping qualities. Wild cranberries are similar in color and shape to the more familiar commercial varieties but they are about half the size. They make up for their small size in flavor, however!

On my first trip to a cranberry bog, I misjudged the distance between two floating mats and jumped instead chest-deep into the mud and water between them. After scrambling on to the mat, I discovered it was too small to support my weight. Gurgling and bubbling, it began to tip and sink. I missed the shore on the return leap. Brrrr! And that mat was covered with cranberries! I returned with hip boots and a board for a bridge and had a good harvest.

Cranberries can be eaten raw but are better cooked in jam or pie, or better still, cranberry sauce. My recipe for cranberry sauce: Crush the berries and then boil them in just enough water to float them in the pot. After a few minutes of cooking, add honey to sweeten. Then boil again. When the mixture becomes thick enough to be called sauce, it's ready.

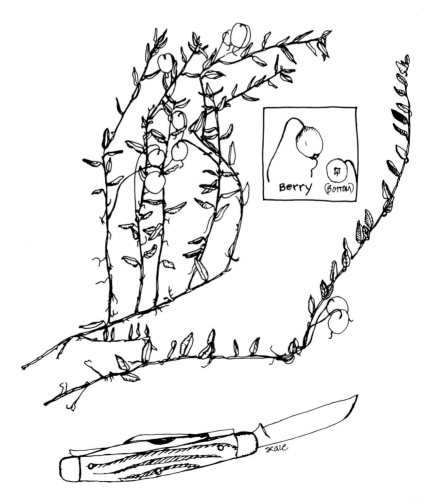

Berry (Bottom)

scale

Wild Tiger Lily, *Lilium columbianum*

The tiger lily is a tall lily with its leaves mostly in whorls. In the summer, its nodding orange flowers are very conspicuous. They are usually deep orange red and are strongly marked with dark purple spots. The petals turn backward to expose the delicate inner parts.

Tiger lilies are found in gravelly, well-drained open woods and on exposed hillsides from near sea level to three or four thousand feet in altitude. The plants grow from two to four feet tall. Because of the shortened growing season and heavy snows of the high country, they become progressively smaller and bloom later as the altitude increases.

Tiger lilies are not plentiful, but they are common enough to warrant occasional use. The scaly bulb, or corm, is the edible portion of the plant. These bulbs may be dug at any season but to do so will destroy the whole plant. Therefore, for conservation's sake, dig the bulbs in the fall after the plant has bloomed, produced seeds and withered. This gives the plant a chance to reproduce itself and, also, the bulbs are fattest at this time. Look for the large seed capsule atop a swaying or broken brown stalk and then dig at the base of the stalk.

To prepare for eating, cut the roots away from the bulb. Pull the flower stalk free and thoroughly wash the flaky bulb. While they are edible raw, they are much better either boiled whole or chopped and fried. The bulbs have a pleasant flavor, a bit like wild rice. Being quite starchy, the bulbs do well in stews and casseroles, or as a substitute for potatoes.

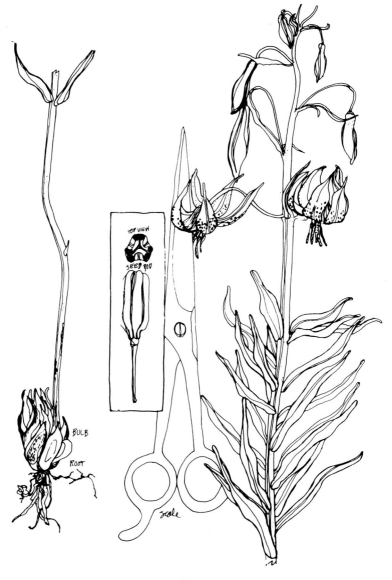

TOP VIEW

SEED POD

BULB

ROOT

scale

Some Words of Caution

In the course of writing this book I have found several plants which are considered edible in many of the older books but now seem to be toxic. Some of the more important ones found within the range of this book are listed below.

Bracken fern *(Pteridium aquilinum)* has long been considered edible. The literature cites several tribes of Pacific Northwestern Indians who traditionally used this plant for food. It is eaten in Japan where this plant also grows. Recent studies have indicated that the consumption of bracken in large amounts or over long periods of time may be related to stomach cancer. The studies are not yet conclusive and may be relative to soil type, water quality or other environment factors. (See footnote.)

Skunk cabbage *(Lysichiton americanum)* is rarely eaten today, probably because of its terrible taste. It is said to have been eaten by northwestern Indians to avoid starvation in the very early spring. I have sampled the leaves and roots of this plant raw and cooked several ways. One would have to be almost starving to enjoy or even endure it for long! The plant contains calcium oxalate, a crystaline substance which is highly irritable.

Wild peas *(beach pea)* are said to contain a toxic substance which is cumulative. You may eat small amounts safely but as the amount and/or frequency are increased you may wake up paralyzed or may not wake up at all. None at all is the safest method.

Note:

Roadside spraying of pesticides can also make plants toxic if much of the material is ingested. I would recommend limiting the use of edible plants found within fifty feet of most roads, and limiting to situations of dire need the use of plants mentioned in the cautionary note.

Bracken Fern—Reference Sources

Evans, I.A., "The Radiomimetic Nature of Bracken Toxin."
Cancer Research, 28 (1968): 2252-2261.

Evans, I.A., and J. Mason. "Carcinogenic Activity of Bracken."
Nature, 208 (1965): 913-914.

Hodge, W.A., "Fern Foods of Japan and the Problem of Toxicity."
American Fern Journal 63 (1973): 77-80.

Pamukeu, A.M. and J.M. Price. 1969. "Induction of intestinal and urinary bladder cancer in rats by feeding Bracken fern."
J. Nat. Cancer Inst. 43: 275-281.

Acknowledgments

Few books are totally the work of one man. Many of my ideas were enhanced by the works of others, some of which appear in the bibliography. Many other people assisted me in the preparation of this book, some unknowingly. I would like to express thanks to Peggy Smith for her guile in getting me to start this project; to Scot Taylor, whose darkroom I used during many an odd hour and day; to Richard Conrad, who loaned me the camera, to the late Dr. C. Blazer, for his correction of my botanical language; to Dr. Bob Dale for his lessons in the English language; to my friends of Bainbridge Island and other places who encouraged me, but more importantly, gave me bits and pieces of information and who shared their good cooking with me; and to Hannah Jones, whose fine work appears in these pages. Because of these people, I have grown.

Terry Domico

Afterword

Only recently has the public gained notice that plants are extremely vulnerable to man's disruption of their habitat. They cannot move aside when the plow or bulldozer approaches. If the soil is altered, the plant community is altered. When the soil becomes too dry or wet to meet their needs, plants languish and disappear. Blacktop seals the ground from almost all living things.

Collectors, too, are a hazard to those species which are few in number or very selective about where they live. Plants cannot run and hide. We must live but we must be gentle...to all things. They are part of our life.

Bibliography

Brown, Annora, **Old Man's Garden,** Gray's Publishing, Ltd., Sidney, B.C., 1970.

Gibbons, Euell, **Stalking the Healthful Herbs,** David McKay Company, Inc., New York, N.Y., 1972.

Gibbons, Euell, **Stalking the Wild Asparagus,** David McKay Company, Inc., New York, N.Y. 1970.

Gunther, Erna, **Ethnobotony of Western Washington,** University of Washington Press, Seattle, Washington, 1945.

Hardin, James W., and Arena, Jay M., M.D., **Human Poisoning from Native and Cultivated Plants,** Duke University Press, 1974.

Haskins, Leslie L., **Wildflowers of the Pacific Coast,** Binford and Mort (Second Edition), 1967.

Kirk, Donald R., **Wild Edible Plants of the Western United States,** Naturegraph Publishers, Healdsburg, California, 1970.

Martin, George W., and Scott, Robert W., **Food in the Wilderness,** George W. Martin, Bremerton, Washingon, 1963.

Medsger, Oliver P., **Edible Wild Plants,** University of California Press, Berkeley, California, 1964.

Munz, Philip A., **Shore Wildflowers of California, Oregon and Washington,** 1964.

Saunders, Charles P., **Useful Wild Plants of the U.S. and Canada,** R.M. McBride and Co., New York, N.Y., 1934.

Sharpe, Grant, and Wenonah, **101 Wildflowers of the Olympic National Park,** University of Washington Press, Seattle, Washington, 1963.

Stewart, Charles, **Wildflowers of the Olympics,** Nature Education Enterprises, 1972.

Szcawinshi, Adam F., and Hardy, George A., **Guide to Common Edible Plants of British Columbia,** British Columbia Provincial Museum, Department of Recreation and Conservation.

Underhill, J.E., **Northwestern Wild Berries,** Hancock House Publishers, Saanichton, B.C., 1979.

**FOR A LIST OF NATURE GUIDES
SEND SELF-ADDRESSED STAMPED ENVELOPE
TO THE PUBLISHER.**